Preface

Nautical archaeology often conjures up images of sunken galleons, lost treasures, and perilous adventures far beneath the surface. Scott McGuckin's discovery at Carpow was rather different. It lay at the edge of the Tay Estuary, and when the tide was low all that could be seen was a blackened piece of oak poking out from the mud. Most would have dismissed it as an old tree-trunk carried down by the river, but Scott had seen an ancient dug-out in Dundee Museum and recognised that this was probably another. His perception led to the remarkable archaeological project chronicled by this booklet, and the recovery of a nautical treasure which has transported us into the heart of Bronze Age Scotland.

For as long as humans have inhabited our countryside they have used boats. Bands of Mesolithic hunter-gatherers probing the regenerating landscape left by the receding ice cap almost ten thousand years ago found their way to places in the Hebrides, and off Fife, which they could only have reached in water craft. Many of the earliest vessels were probably of hides stretched over a light framework, but because of their fragile nature no remains of such craft have been found. Boats dug out of a tree-trunk, however, may be just as ancient a tradition, and because of their massive solidity are much more likely to be preserved, especially if encapsulated in wet muddy conditions as at Carpow.

This project is remarkable for the range of skills which the Perth and Kinross Heritage Trust have brought together and co-ordinated. The boat's recovery was a major feat of salvage, made all the more challenging by its fragile waterlogged condition and the need to ensure that every detail, including the environmental evidence locked in the surrounding mud and peat, was meticulously recorded and sampled for analysis. The major task of conservation, without which the boat would have dried out and disintegrated, was carried out in the laboratory of the National Museums of Scotland, where pioneering work on treating the remains of historic wooden vessels has been going on for many years. Through these processes the team has been able to interpret and understand the Carpow boat, and catch glimpses of the people who made and used it. This has led to the building of a reconstruction using replica Bronze Age tools, and testing it in Loch Tay.

For many years Historic Scotland has recognised this country's rich nautical archaeological heritage, and has done much to protect and preserve it. The Carpow dug-out is a major national asset, and a reminder of how important water craft were to past generations until quite recent times. It now has a permanent home in Perth Museum and Art Gallery, and will give visitors, today and in the future, a tantalising glimpse of the very different landscape (and seascape) of Bronze Age Perthshire.

Colin Martin
University of St Andrews

The Carpow Logboat

A Bronze Age vessel brought to life

David Strachan

Perth and Kinross Heritage Trust

Printed and Bound by Farquhar and Son Ltd., Perth

ISBN 978-0-9564427-2-7

PERTH AND KINROSS HERITAGE TRUST

Front cover: The 3,000 year old Carpow logboat and the Loch Tay logboat made in August 2009. Back cover: A reconstruction of the Carpow boat fishing on the Tay Estuary; the stern after excavation, and a replica adze with the Loch Tay boat.

An Introduction...
Logboats from around the World

What are logboats?

Logboats, also known as dugout canoes, are one of the most basic types of boat, with others being made from hides, basketry or bundles of reeds. Put simply, they are boats made from a hollowed tree trunk, and the earliest known watercraft in the world. The earliest known examples are from Pesse in the Netherlands and Noyen-sur-Seine in France, and were fashioned from pine logs in the 7th to 8th millennium BC, as soon after the last Ice Age that sizeable trees are believed to have grown in north-west Europe. Logboats also have a remarkable distribution, however, having been made around the world wherever trees of sufficient size have grown, and it is likely that they developed from floating logs in different places at different times. Given this 10,000 year history of logboat manufacture, it is astonishing that they are still made and used by people today in various parts of the world. Very few objects have been produced and used in the same way for such extended periods of time. Simple logboats are made by removing the bark and sapwood from a log and then hollowing out the interior while shaping the ends and outside. Complex logboats are where additional fittings are added, such as planks along each side to increase freeboard (the distance between the water and the top of the boat), internal volume and stability. Such fittings can allow logboats to carry greater loads and to be used in rougher waters, even outwith the rivers and estuaries to which they are best suited.

Logboats, including paired examples with sails, greet Captain Cook ship in Karakakooa Bay, Hawai'i Island (from Bankes' "Geography" of 1797: AK Bell Library, Local Studies Department).

The earliest known logboat from Britain is the fragment of an oak vessel from Catherinefield, Dumfries and Galloway, dated to around 2000 BC. There is a common misconception that all logboats are prehistoric, however, whereas in fact the majority of British logboats date between around AD 1000-1300, with prehistoric examples being relatively rare. Further, while there are records of many hundreds of logboats from the British Isles, the vast majority were discovered in a very poor state of preservation. Indeed, many were found in the 19th century and no longer survive at all, and so of the records of over 150 logboats from Scotland, only about 30 actually survive, either in museums or left where they were discovered. The subject of this publication, the Late Bronze Age Carpow logboat, is not only one of the oldest boats known from Scotland, but also one of the best preserved from the British Isles and Ireland.

The story that follows begins with the discovery of the Carpow vessel, continues through the excavation and recovery. It then looks at the process of conservation and turns full circle to describe the manufacture of the most recent Scottish logboat, inspired by Carpow and made using replica Bronze Age tools on Loch Tay in 2009. Finally, we will consider how the boat was used, and what it can tell us about life in the Late Bronze Age in Tayside.

Tales of the River Bank:
a Prehistoric Boat from the Tay

Discovery and evaluation

The logboat from Carpow Bank, near Abernethy on the Tay Estuary, was first reported by metal-detectorist Scott McGuckin in August 2001. He recognised that the timber, partially buried in the inter-tidal mudflats, was a boat; rather than just an eroding tree trunk, of which there are many on the bank. He reported to *The Scotsman* "I have only been doing this for a few months and can't believe this find" and subsequently explained that he recognised the boat having seen the example in Dundee Museum. Shortly after this, a small team of archaeologists from Perth and Kinross Heritage Trust, Historic Scotland, the National Museums of Scotland and Perth Museum and Art Gallery visited the site and confirmed that the find was indeed a logboat. A plan was then developed to assess the importance of the boat, both in terms of logboat studies and the archaeology of the area, asking four key questions: how old was the boat? how long was it? what was the condition of the buried portion of the vessel? and how should it be protected while its was being considered?

The first question was easily answered through radiocarbon dating and by November that year, a date for the boat was confirmed in the range of 1260-910 BC. This established the boat as being around 3,000 years old, from the Late Bronze Age, and as being one of the earliest boats from Scotland – clearly worthy of further study. The remaining questions of how long the boat was, and what its overall condition was, would require some investigation through excavation. From the outset, however, it was clear that this would be no ordinary archaeological dig. The inter-tidal flats can be accessed only during the lowest tides, and only when there was minimal flow of water carried by the rivers Tay and Earn. The correct conditions occurred for only 4-5 days during each batch of twice-monthly spring-tides between June and August, but even then, the site was only exposed for short periods of 3-4 hours. Excavation itself was hampered by the daily re-covering of the site with sand, mud and gravel carried by the tide, and also by flooding during excavations, which required the use of motorised pumps. As a result, the team had to work rapidly in short bursts of well-planned activity, re-excavating much of what had been uncovered the day before: a process of two steps forward and one step back...

The logboat in 2001 and during evaluation excavations in 2002.

The first excavations, carried out in October 2002, aimed to assess the condition of the exposed section, assumed to be the bow. It was confirmed that while much of the exposed end had been lost through abrasion from sand carried in the water over the years, this had occurred much less on the buried hull. In July 2003, a second excavation established the full length of the vessel to be around 9m. For only a few minutes, just long enough to allow photography and basic measurements to be taken, the buried stern was revealed for the first time in 3,000 years. This was found to be in an excellent state of preservation, and confirmed that Carpow was not only a very early logboat, but that it was the best preserved ever found in Scotland.

After these initial small-scale excavations, the vessel was re-buried and covered with sandbags to protect it from further erosion. Its condition was then monitored while consideration was given to whether the boat should be excavated, or whether it could be preserved *in situ*; in the mud where it was found, probably through continued sand-bagging. By 2004, however, it was clear that the latter was not a long-term option and plans were developed for excavation, recovery, conservation and display. With part-funding from Historic Scotland, Perth and Kinross Heritage Trust took on the task of excavating and recovering the boat, with plans for conservation of the vessel by the

The excellent preservation of the stern of the boat was briefly glimpsed in 2003.

National Museums of Scotland, and eventual display at Perth Museum and Art Gallery. By 2005, funding was secured and plans completed to overcome the considerable logistical challenges of the recovery for the summer of 2006.

Tide and time: digging a hole in the Firth of Tay

The aim of the 2006 project was to excavate the logboat; to collect and record any associated artefacts; to study the ancient peat deposits and tree stumps found on the bank; and to recover the vessel and transport it to the National Museums of Scotland in Edinburgh. Work was carried out in seven days over two tidal windows in July and August 2006, and involved excavating deposits around and beneath the logboat, while recording and recovering associated deposits and finds as conditions allowed.

The fully excavated boat awaiting recovery.

This process was carried out in two stages: the excavation of the interior and exterior of the exposed bow of the boat; and subsequently of the buried stern, supporting the excavated boat on sandbags until it was eventually freed from the bank. While water pumps were used during the excavation, the site was submerged at each high tide, re-covering the boat in sediments that had to be removed in the following session.

The full size of the boat is revealed for the first time.

During the excavation, the team also studied the peat and surviving ancient tree-stumps found on the surface of the bank. Both the peats and the oak and birch tree stumps were found to date to around 8200-7700 BC, much earlier than the logboat. The trees had grown along what was then one of several braided river channels, and during their lifetime, local conditions became wet enough for peat to form as a result of the decomposition of marsh and other salt tolerant plants. A study of the diatoms (microscopic algae) within the silts confirmed they had formed in estuarine waters. While little could be gleaned from the mixed gravels of the bank, into which the boat had gradually sank over the centuries, some early organic rich deposits did survive inside and beneath the boat. These water-logged, black muddy deposits contained masses of small fragments of twigs from brushwood, hazelnuts shells, and pieces of possibly worked wood, laid down inside the boat after it went out of use. The worked wood included what may have been a toggle, and a small wooden stake, possibly a piece of a basket. Both the wooden objects and the hazelnut shells were dated and found to be contemporary with the logboat. The hazelnut shells were a food source that would have been gathered from mature hazel woodland in the autumn, and the cache found inside the Carpow logboat had been nibbled by the common or hazel dormouse, which left distinct tooth-marks on four of the shells

The tabulated peat on the bank.

The final journey

Following excavation, the vessel was rigged to float by inserting three 200 litre plastic barrels within the hull, a process overseen by conservation staff from the National Museums of Scotland, who confirmed that the boat was robust enough to undergo the operation. Once in position, the barrels were partially filled with water to decrease buoyancy, allowing control over the upward lift, and the vessel was floated on the incoming flood tide. Once clear of the excavation trench, it was guided to a temporary location on a nearby mud bank beside the reed beds near the estuary shore.

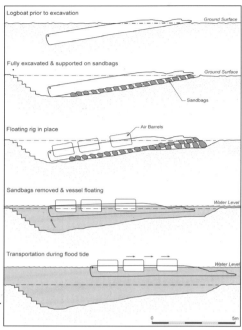

The process of lifting and floating the boat with air filled barrels.

The flood tide moves the air-filled boat for the first time in 3,000 years.

A mud-pack is applied to boat to stop it drying out in the hot summer sun.

The vessel remained anchored there overnight, during the high tide, and was finally fully revealed, for the first time, with the falling tide the following morning. The boat was then de-rigged to allow a full photographic record to be made and a mud-pack was applied to prevent it from drying out over the next seven hours in the hot summer sun. By late afternoon the vessel had been re-rigged to float for the second time and on the next flood tide was once again floated and then towed in slack water by a small power-boat, at slow speed, the 3 km or so to Newburgh. On arrival at the quay, the dive team guided the floating vessel into a 9.3m long steel box lifting-frame, and the frame and the boat was lifted by crane onto a waiting flatbed lorry. While the project had developed over five years, the lift from water to dry land took only three nerve-racking minutes. The logboat was then transported to the National Museums of Scotland to begin the process of conservation and another journey began: the detailed study of the boat, and the task of appreciating what it meant to both logboat studies, and our understanding of Bronze Age Tayside.

The floating boat is prepared for the tow.

The Carpow Logboat

The dive team insert the vessel within the lifting frame.

Hanging within the frame, the boat is lifted from the water onto a flatbed lorry.

The boat and frame are prepared for the drive to Edinburgh.

Conserving Carpow
for the Future...

Once within the conservation laboratory of the National Museums of Scotland, the process of conservation, that would stabilise its condition and preserve it for future generations, began. The wood had only survived the last 3,000 years because it had remained waterlogged in anaerobic conditions, where the lack of oxygen in the water restricts decay. As waterlogged oak gradually decays, however, wood polymers are replaced by water, until there is eventually less wood and more water. Carpow, as is usual for waterlogged ancient oak, had a sound core with a degraded outer layer. Without conservation treatment, this outer layer would have shrunk by as much as 60% by volume, and would have destroyed the surface of the artefact.

Inspecting the bottom of the logboat in Edinburgh.

During the initial stages of cleaning and recording, the vessel was simply kept wet, however, in order to make it stable enough for display and long-term storage, a waxy polymer called Polyethylene glycol (PEG) was impregnated into the wood to replace the water. While various options, including spraying PEG onto the surface of the boat, were considered, it was decided to submerge the boat within specially made PEG tanks, and to freeze dry the timber, where the water was turned into ice and removed as water vapour within a vacuum. This process controversially involved cutting the boat into three sections. The decision was confidently made, however, in the light of other logboat conservation projects in Britain, which have run into significant difficulties by using other methods. The Carpow conservation process was a pragmatic response which assured a result within years rather than decades.

Experts also studied the tree-rings in the hope of securing a more accurate date through dendrochronology, where patterns in annual growth rings can determine an individual year. The removal of the internal heartwood of the log limited the number of tree-rings available however, and so additional radiocarbon dates were taken from different parts of the boat. A final problem for the conservation team was that the gravel concretions adhered to the surface of the vessel contained iron and sulfur compounds which can oxidise in air to produce sulfuric acid. This is problem recognised internationally in marine conservation, and research is ongoing by the National Museums of Scotland and the Mary Rose Trust to develop solutions. While the conservation of the logboat is still in process at the time of writing, it is planned for completion by mid-2010, prior to initial display at Perth Museum and Art Gallery in 2011.

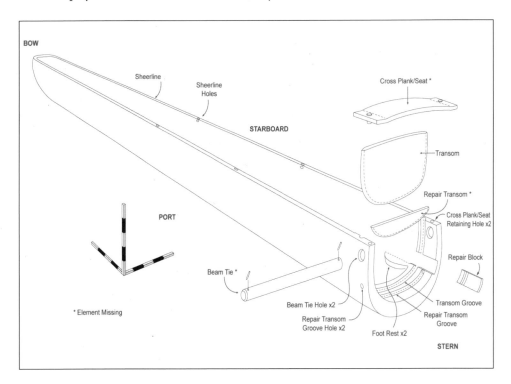

The main elements of the Carpow logboat and terms referred to in the text.

Bringing the Boat to Life:
the Loch Tay Project

Our understanding of prehistoric logboats has increased significantly in recent decades by experimental work using replica prehistoric tools to reconstruct how such boats were made. In August 2009, Perth and Kinross Heritage Trust, in partnership with the Scottish Crannog Centre, reconstructed a prehistoric logboat, in the spirit of the Carpow, as an educational project. The main concession was that a Douglas Fir log was used, rather than oak, as tall straight oak trees of this diameter are extremely rare in Britain. Many of the features from Carpow were incorporated, and a combination of modern and replica Late Bronze Age tools was used and the boat was hollowed completely by hand using the same processes that the Bronze Age boat builders would have used. The project was carried out by Perth and Kinross Heritage Trust staff, with the aid of volunteers and students, under the instruction of ancient wood-working expert Damian Goodburn. In addition to learning how to haft and use the replica socketted axe-heads, specially cast for the project by bronze sword-smith Neil Burridge, the team eventually launched the boat and tested it on the water, eventually paddling it across Loch Tay to the Scottish Crannog Centre where it now resides.

The following begins by looking at the tools used, and then describes each stage of manufacture, illustrated with reconstruction drawings of Carpow, and photographs from the Loch Tay project.

The Late Bronze Age toolkit

Stone axes had been used to make oak logboats since at least 2000 BC in Scotland, and probably for thousands of years before that. And while the overall processes involved did not change very much, the new metal tools of the Bronze Age allowed more advanced wood-working, and we will begin by looking at the tools available to the Carpow boat builders.

The variety of edged tools available in the Late Bronze Age was small, with the principle tool being socketted axe-heads, hafted in line with the handle as axes, and transversely as adzes. These have rounded edges between around 40-50mm in width, smaller than both the Neolithic axes that preceded them and the Iron Age axes that followed. It is difficult to explain the decrease in blade size of the larger tools during the Bronze Age and compared to modern axes, the Late Bronze Age examples seem impractically light and small, but once the user has adjusted to their different feel and gained some experience, they are very efficient.

Early and Middle Bronze Age and axes were cast in open stone, or clay impression moulds. The major development in mould technology in the Late Bronze Age saw the casting of hollow sections as found in socketted axes, but also in socketted spears and gouges. This involved the use of separate clay cores within stone and bronze moulds. It is likely that bronze smiths would have made many axes in one session with many pre-made clay cores, which would guide the molten bronze through feedholes into the hollow section in the mould. Bronze smiths were skilled specialists of the time and once cast, axes, swords and other tools would have been transported far afield as gifts and through trade.

Making the haft from a branch and section of trunk: this gives the tool strength and also some additional weight.

The Carpow Logboat

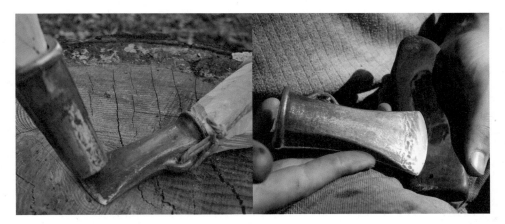

A socketted bronze hardening hammer is used to produce a working edge (left) and a whetstone used to sharpen the edge (right).

Various materials, including twisted flax and hide, were used to fasten the socketted axes.

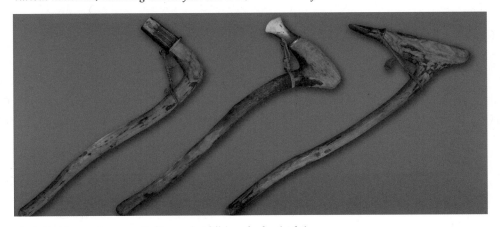

Socketted bronze hammer (left), axe (middle) and adze (right).

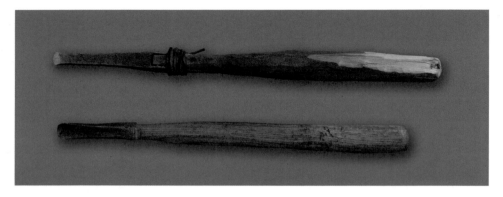

Smaller metal edge tools: chisel (above) and gouge (below).

On Loch Tay, it was found that bronze tools generally required re-sharpening roughly three times more often than modern steel edged hand tools. It was also interesting to note that the technique for use was very different: the lighter replica tools requiring a pecking action, using more forearm work, rather than a swinging action. Indeed the team found that they developed two sets of blisters in slightly different places – one set from the modern tools and another from the bronze ones!

As important as the metal tools were the numerous wooden tools, principally dry, seasoned wedges, for cleaving surplus wood away, and mauls and clubs to hammer them. In addition, poles, log bearers, and skid logs needed to move the log and roughed out boat, and additional aids such as a string lines and pigments for marking, such as charcoal, would also have been required as they were on Loch Tay.

Wooden wedges and the large wooden maul (hammer) used on Loch Tay.

After the three week project on Loch Tay it was clear to the team that perhaps the most important resources that the Bronze Age boat builders had were their skill, experience and muscle…

Using a socketted axe hafted as an adze on the Loch Tay boat.

Selecting a suitable tree

The remains of the Carpow logboat measured 8.9m; however, with its bow intact it would have been around 10m in length. The oak tree from which the boat was fashioned has been estimated to have been around 400 years old, with a straight trunk of at least 12m and a total height of around 30m. Unlike oak trees grown in the open, oaks grown in the ancient dark woodland grew tall and straight, with a high branching point. Such trees are extremely rare in Britain today, although they do exist in the forest reserves of Poland. Oaks of this age and size almost always suffer from 'brittle heart' rot, which begins low down at the base of the tree and spreads upwards into the bole. This is why oak logboats have separate transoms fitted at the stern (see page 18).

Selecting a good straight tree, with few branches or knots, to make a boat of the desired size may well have had a ritual dimension or have associated ceremonies before or after the felling, both of which are recorded in ethnographic accounts. For example, in some cultures the boat building team is led by a high status, priest-like master builder, while in others simply an older man with experience. Recently the Ye'kwana people of south-western Venezuela have been recorded as collecting handfuls of seed from the parent tree to plant "for the future"…

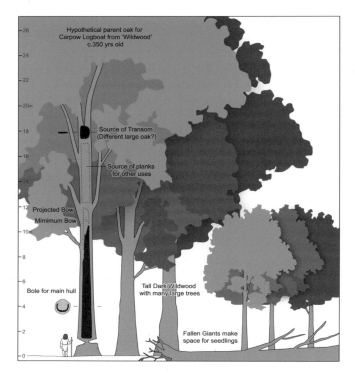

Carpow shown within its parent oak tree.

An experienced elder selects a tree.

The Carpow Logboat

Modern foresters fell trees with chainsaws by a cut near to the ground, using a lower 'V' shaped 'drop' cut to help direct the fall of the tree. In prehistory, the 'V' cut was also used, though it was made much higher up for ease of swinging the axe, and to avoid the flared buttress near the ground. Removing the hard, dust-impregnated oak bark would have dulled the small bronze axes quickly and they would have required regular sharpening until fresh green timber was exposed.

Two V-shaped cuts are made to control the fall of the tree.

A boat from a log - the restricted hull

The overall shape of a logboat is determined by the parent log, and is gradually revealed, like a sculpture, through the below process. This would have taken as many as ten people three to four weeks to manufacture, representing a considerable investment in time and labour.

A photomosaic of the 8.9m long boat.

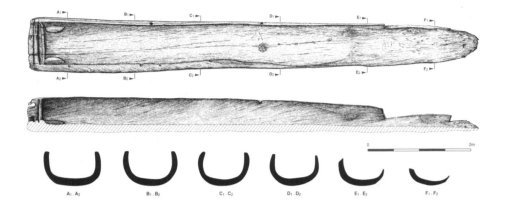

Scale drawings of the 8.9m long boat.

The shape of a boat is gradually teased out of the log on Loch Tay.

The Carpow Logboat

The missing bow

As the bow of Carpow had been lost to erosion, a number of possible reconstructions were considered: rectangular; rounded; and pointed. Evidence from broadly comparable contemporary logboats, suggests that a simple rounded shape is most likely. Logboats with elongated bows and animal figureheads are known from logboat using communities today, however and are suggested for four early Scottish oak logboats: Loch Arthur, Dumfries and Galloway (13.7m long/dated to c150 BC-AD 200); Loch of Kinnordy, Angus (c4.6m long/dated cAD 735); Buston, North Ayrshire (6.7m long/probably cAD 50-500); and the Errol 2 vessel, which is 8.9m long, and has a pointed bow with a "rude but forcible resemblance to the head of an animal". Errol 2, also from the Tay Estuary, is dated to the 6th century AD and is on display at The McManus: Dundee's Art Gallery and Museum.

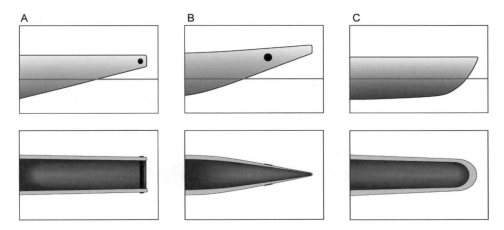

Possible forms of bow for Carpow: C being the most likely.

The simple rounded bow on Loch Tay takes shape.

Removing the branches and cutting to length

Once the tree was felled, the first job involved cutting the log to length and the removal of side branches. The log used for Carpow, which at this stage would have weighed around 9.5 tonnes, was largely free of large branches, with the first major knot, left by a medium sized branch, being around 7.3m above the ground.

Lopping the branches and cutting the log to length.

Removing the bark, sapwood and 'waste' timber

It is probable that the bottom and outside of the hull was completed first, with the log then being rolled over to allow the top and inside of the boat to be worked on. The main process of removing unwanted bulk timber, by cutting grooves and then splitting off timber between them, was then undertaken. This controlled splitting and cleaving off of large blocks of timber is far quicker and more efficient than removing timber chip by chip, and minimising the use of valuable bronze tools at the expense of easily replaceable wooden wedges and 'mauls' (hammers).

Removing large planks using bronze axes to make V-shaped cuts and wooden wedges and mauls to cleave off the timber.

Removing the first plank from the Loch Tay boat with wedges: the slow grown oak of Carpow would have split much better than this fast grown Douglas Fir.

Smoothing the external hull

The next stage was to remove the sapwood from the sides of the log and to finish what would be the bottom of the boat. The outer hull would have been made relatively smooth and fair though gentle paring blows with adzes and axes. It is likely that animal fat or fish oil would have been smeared on the hull at this point, to slow down drying and reduce splitting.

Smoothing the bottom and sides of the vessel.

Removing the bark and sapwood from the sides of the vessel.

Loch Tay and the finished bottom of the boat, treated with vegetable oil.

Halfway there: rolling the log

At this stage, with the bottom and the lower parts of the sides completed, stout poles were employed to roll the partly formed hull onto its bottom. The Carpow boat-to-be would have weighed in the region of 8 tonnes at this point, and would have taken as many as ten people with the aid of timber debris chocks and fulcrums to control the movement. The much lighter log on Loch Tay still required similar numbers to manoeuvre onto bearer logs, raising the base slightly off the ground.

Rolling the completed bottom of the partly formed hull onto bearer logs.

The smaller (and lighter) log is rolled on Loch Tay.

Splitting off unwanted timber to the sheerline

Once rolled over the process of removing timber from the intended sheerline (the top) of the boat was once again carried out by cutting grooves and splitting out blocks of timber with wedges.

Removing blocks of timber from what will be the top of the boat.

Marking out the hull shape

With the unwanted timber removed, the shape of the top of the boat could be marked out, probably using charcoal, by an experienced boat-maker.

Using charcoal to mark out the sheerline on Loch Tay.

Marking out the finished line of the hull sides and both bow and stern shapes.

Hollowing out the interior

It is commonly thought that fire was always used in the process of hollowing out logboats, however there is no evidence for this in logboats from Britain. In other parts of the world fire has, and continues, to be used to soften thin hulls and allow them to be pushed apart to maximise the internal volume of the boat and so increase stability. Large blocks of fresh oak are virtually fire retardant, however, and the boats must have been made while the wood was 'green', as allowed to dry it would spilt and crack and become too hard to shape with hand tools. In the Carpow boat, very faint vertical 'in cuts' survive which indicate the V-shaped grooves cut to allow groove and splinter hollowing, removing blocks of wood with wedges as on the top and bottom of the log.

Hollowing out of the hull with wedges and mauls.

The log begins to take on the shape of a boat once the interior is hollowed out.

Finishing the hull

The final stage of thinning out the hull would have involved carefully cutting shallow scores to the desired thickness and then smoothing off the surface of the boat with gentle blows of an adze blade.

Finishing off the hull with the gentle paring action of axes and adzes.

Sheerline holes

On the Carpow boat, three enigmatic holes were found carved through the top of the sheerline to the inside of the hull. Such features very rarely survive on prehistoric logboats as the tops of the hull are usually lost to erosion. It is likely that there were more of these, regularly spaced in pairs, and while we cannot be absolutely sure what they were for, an imprint survives on the inboard face one of the holes suggesting that a 'loose toggle' straddled hole as a fastening for an external lashing. It is possible that this held down a spray deck of skin covers, which would have been very useful in a fairly unstable vessel with a low freeboard, protecting cargo and minimising incoming water. It has also been suggested that they may have acted as rowlocks for oars. These neat oval holes, around 40mm in diameter, were clearly carved using finer bronze tools such as gouges and chisels.

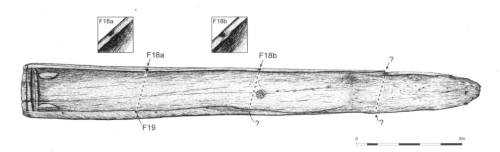

A sheerline hole showing a loose toggle fitting.

The stern

The well-preserved stern of the Carpow boat was by far the most complicated part of the vessel. The boat builders needed to insert a separate transom, or back-end, because of the heartwood rot running from the base of the tree and, as in other examples, this was fitted into a U-shaped groove. In addition to this transom, other features indicated where lost fixtures and fittings had once been, and comparison with other examples proved invaluable for understanding these (see page 18). Carving the fittings at the stern required the most complex workmanship and the use of chisels and gouges in addition to axes and adzes. It was also possible to see that the stern of the boat developed over time with repairs and alterations being made.

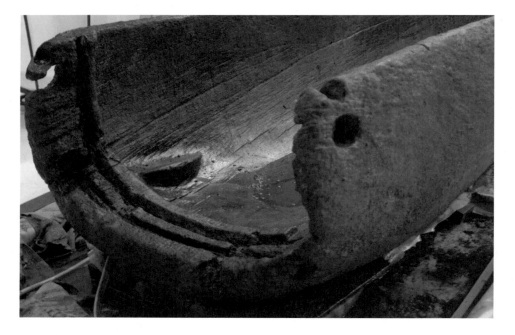

The Carpow stern showing transom grooves, footrests and beam-tie holes.

Transom

The Carpow transom is a substantial piece of oak, measuring 0.6m in height and 0.85m in width and tree-ring studies have shown that it was fashioned by cleaving a plank tangentially from part of the crown of a large tree, high up where the tree bole forked into the two main branches of the trunk. It is impossible to say from the tree-rings, or from radiocarbon dating, whether the transom came from the same parent tree of the hull or whether it came from a different tree at a later date, however. The well-preserved toolmarks that survived over the entire inboard face of the transom reflect a rougher level of finishing than on the hull itself and may suggest that the surviving transom is a replacement.

The transom groove is marked out and carved out with a chisel.

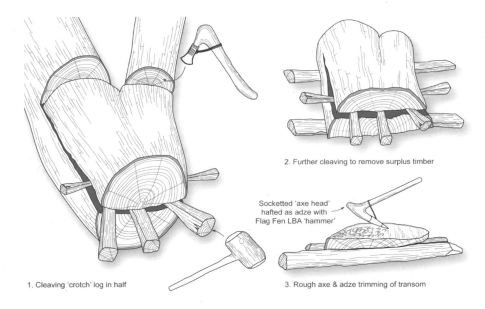

2. Further cleaving to remove surplus timber

Socketted 'axe head' hafted as adze with Flag Fen LBA 'hammer'

1. Cleaving 'crotch' log in half

3. Rough axe & adze trimming of transom

The transom was carved from a 'crotch' log: the fork of two main branches.

The size and shape of the toolmarks also indicated that the blade of the axe used to finish the surface of the transom was around 53mm in length, the average size of Late Bronze Age axe finds from Scotland. The toolmarks included jam features, where the strike has been unsuccessful and the blade became stuck in the wood, and tool signatures, where distinctive pattern of small ridges, created by nicks in the blade of a tool, were left on the worked surface. These features offered a tantalising insight, and direct link to the Late Bronze Age wood-worker: even indicating the direction in which the craftsman had worked.

The transom with its toolmarks showing the direction of work.

Making the stern water-tight

To water-proof the transom into its groove, a 'caulking' of moss and carpentry waste was rammed into the groove. The moss was identified as *Rhytidiadelphus squarrosus* or 'Springy Turf-moss', a common moss of grassland, heathland and upland woods. This would have been dried then inserted into the groove before the transom was fitted, so that it would expand when wet to promote a seal. The technique was replicated on Loch Tay.

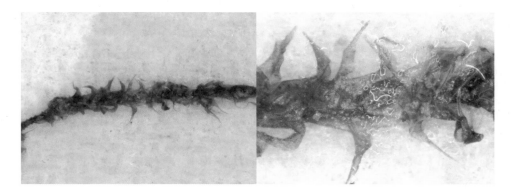

3,000 year old moss caulking from the Carpow transom groove.

Loch Tay: moss caulking is fitted along the transom groove.

Loch Tay: the transom is inserted and the sheerline finished with a modern adze.

The Carpow Logboat

Footrests

One feature which appears unique to Carpow is the pair of footrests inboard at the stern, carved out of the parent log itself. As the floor of the hull is curved transversely, it would have been awkward to stand in for long periods of time, and difficult to achieve stability and grip. The boat-builders solution offered the helmsman a sound and level platform, standing with one foot on each footrest, while punting, steering or directing the craft. The slight additional height would have afforded them a view over the heads of other crew and a commanding position from which to steer, while keeping their feet dry! The footrests also provided a way to balance the logboat, which would have had a tendency to roll starboard to port side, by applying weight on either footrest to make minor adjustments to counter-balance this movement. These ideas were tested and verified on Loch Tay as similar footrests were incorporated into the vessel.

Carving the Loch Tay footrests with an adze (left) and their proposed use while punting the Carpow boat.

A reconstructed seat

A pair of retaining sockets cut into the sheerline of the stern suggests a seat fitted above the transom. The seat would also help to hold the transom down into its groove, acting against the pressure of water while afloat. In addition to this practical function, the seat, like the footrests, appears to be designed for comfort, and would have been valuable on long, slow journeys, or even as a platform to stand on should additional height be required, for example when punting in shallow water.

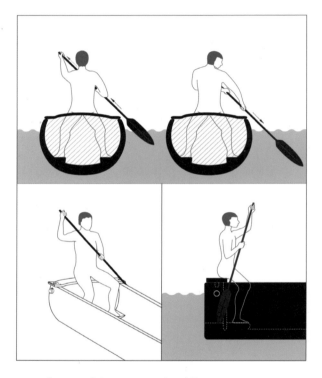

Using the seat while steering and paddling.

The missing beam-tie

A beam-tie is another lost feature implied by fittings in the hull, in this case a pair of circular holes cut horizontally through the sides of the vessel at the top of the stern outboard of the transom. An excellent parallel for these was found in the Iron Age Hasholme logboat from the Humber estuary, where a round-wood timber was fitted through the holes. This would help to pull the two sides of the craft together, and prevent the natural tendency for the sides of the hull to splay out.

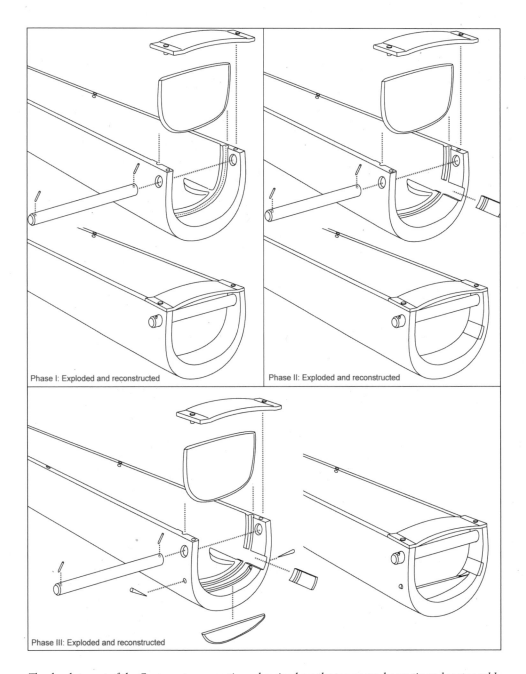

Phase I: Exploded and reconstructed

Phase II: Exploded and reconstructed

Phase III: Exploded and reconstructed

The development of the Carpow stern over time: showing how the transoms, beam tie and seat would have functioned.

Launching the boat

It is estimated that the Carpow boat would have weighed around 1.3 tonnes when newly made, and could have been man-handled on wetted round-wood skid logs by about 10 men. On Loch Tay the boat was made close to the loch-side, and with some effort the 9m long hull was manoeuvred down-slope into the water for the first time…

Rolling the Loch Tay boat towards the water on skid logs.

The boat approaches the loch…

…and is launched.

Crossing Loch Tay in Scotland's latest logboat!

A Bronze Age vessel brought to life

The life of a logboat and the need for repairs

A large oak logboat could have a life of 25-30 years and a number of repairs carried out to Carpow testify to this while reflecting the value of the boat to its owners. The larger of the two splits in the bottom of the hull had seven patches of fat- or oil-saturated plant matter applied. At the stern, a small wooden block was found fitted between the inside of the hull and the transom, probably replacing an area of rotten wood in the parent log. Finally, a smaller transom was fitted outboard of the main transom, probably another response to leakage through the splits in the bottom of the hull, after this wooden block had been fitted. The basal splits were clearly a continuing cause of concern for the Carpow boatmen, and indeed may have been instrumental in the decision to abandon or deliberately sink a boat which was otherwise in good condition.

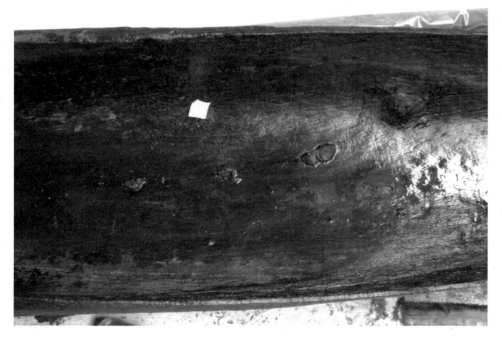

The basal split along the bottom of the hull with repair patches.

Carpow and Late Bronze Age Tayside

The landscape and its people

The Late Bronze Age (around 1200 BC–700 BC) is well known as a period of change, with a shift in settlement types and changes in ritual and funerary traditions with a backdrop of deteriorating climatic conditions. While woodland clearance had begun in the Neolithic (around 4000-2000 BC) human impact on woodland through the Scottish Bronze Age was small-scale and temporary, although in lowland Tayside some settlement may have been longer-term. While pollen records suggest increased grazing from the second millennium onwards, with cultivated increasing from c1500BC, even by 1000 BC woodland cover was still dominant on the well-drained, fertile plains of Tayside covering perhaps as much as 70% of the landscape. These natural woodlands were dominated by deciduous trees such as oak, elm, ash and hazel. We can envisage small dispersed settlements within this wooded landscape, and burning may have been used to control and maintain larger areas for grazing livestock. Around 1000 BC, however, a fairly abrupt deterioration in climate appears to have resulted in the abandonment of many upland settlements, with slightly colder wetter weather.

Ironically we know more about death in the earlier part of the Bronze Age than we do about life: there are complex and shifting burial traditions involving individual burials of both inhumations and cremations with larger cemeteries in use over long periods of time. A recurring theme of Late Bronze Age funerary practice is the re-use of older ritual monuments of Neolithic and earlier Bronze Age, as evidenced at North Mains in Strathearn, although there appears to be generally fewer sites. It is possible that funerary practices changed again and left little, if any, physical trace, for example the deposition of cremations in rivers, in a similar way to the Ganges in India. The possibility of a culture of depositing the dead in a sacred river Tay is all the more credible in light of the valuable contemporary metalwork also deposited at that time and discussed below.

Bronze Age settlements were typically single timber-framed roundhouses with attached enclosures and paddocks for arable cultivation and animal husbandry. Occasionally small clusters existed, and the well preserved remains of many of these can be found parts of highland Perthshire today. The warmer weather of the Bronze Age 'climatic optimum' made settlement at such altitudes more tenable, and the lesser tree cover there, compared with the rich fertile glen floors, may have made arable farming easier to establish. Upland sites tend to be better preserved than their lowland equivalents both because of their more durable construction and because the lowland examples have usually been ploughed away from the middle ages on. As a result of this, more is known about lowlands sites, however, it is probable that Bronze Age settlement in Tayside was ubiquitous across upland and lowland areas.

The rivers Tay and Earn weave around Moncrieffe hill and showing both lowland and highland: the forts on the top of which may have their origins as far back as the Late Bronze Age.

Tayside is particularly rich in open settlements, buildings without a surrounding defensive ditch or palisade, and while enclosed settlements do exist, they are far fewer than in comparable parts of Scotland, such as East Lothian. The relationship between these settlement types remains ambiguous, however, as they are primarily known only as outline plans recorded on air photographs and very few have been excavated and dated. It is possible however that there was shift to more enclosed settlement towards the end of the Bronze Age, perhaps related to the declining climate. Indeed it is possible that the earliest enclosing of hilltops occurred in the Late Bronze Age, suggesting the development of the hill-forts that would dominate settlement in the Iron Age.

The other major restriction to lowland settlement, however, was wetland: peat bogs on the glen floors and coastal salt-marsh that would remain largely un-drained until the medieval period and beyond. This explains the lack of settlement in low-lying areas of Strathearn and the Carse of Gowrie, while clusters of settlements, such as at Straiton; Leuchars; St Madoes; Errol and Invergowrie occurred on raised 'islands' of higher ground. As we will see, such watery places were of special significance to the Late Bronze Age population and were often used for ceremonies involving casting bronze and other objects into the water. The ultimate watercourse in the area, the river Tay has a very clear signature of this intriguing aspect of Late Bronze Age culture...

Late Bronze Age metalwork from the Tay - a sacred river?

An important glimpse of Late Bronze Age life can be gained through an assemblage of contemporary metalwork recovered from the River Tay itself. The finds include five, possibly six, swords; two spearheads; three socketted axe-heads; a sickle and a gouge, all made of bronze.

While the swords were found in the 19th century AD, and so details of where they came from can be vague, there is clearly a concentration from between Perth and Mugdrum Island by Newburgh. The earliest example, found at Mugdrum in 1889, is a superb 11th century BC Limehouse-type sword, a regional variant of a class of flange-hilted swords found across the continent. While none of the rivets which would have held the organic hilt plates in place survive, it is in excellent condition, suggesting loss or deliberate deposition when fully serviceable. Further, the fine Wilburton-type sword recovered in 1854 from the river at Seggieden, on the north bank opposite Elcho, had also been deposited in excellent condition, suggesting that they were offered to the river in a ritual or ceremony.

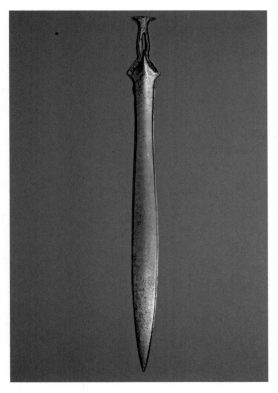

The Late Bronze Age Wilburton-type sword from Seggieden, on the north bank of the Tay opposite Elcho (© Perth Museum & Art Gallery, Perth & Kinross Council).

Similar votive offerings, in much larger quantities, are known from other major east-coast rivers, notably the Thames and the Trent, and are part of a wider culture of deposition of metalwork in watery places, such as bogs, rivers and lochs. Further a number of finds from earlier in prehistory, including Late Neolithic carved stone balls and Early Bronze Age shaft-hole implements known as battle-axes, may suggest that this tradition of offering objects to the river was already long established by the time of the logboat.

Finally, it is thought-provoking to consider that some of the bronze objects from the Tay, such as the socketted axeheads and gouges, were the very type of tools used to make the logboat, and raises the possibility that they may even have been deposited in the river from the boat itself.

A selection of axe-heads, of the type used to make the logboat, probably ritually deposited in the Tay (© National Museums Scotland).

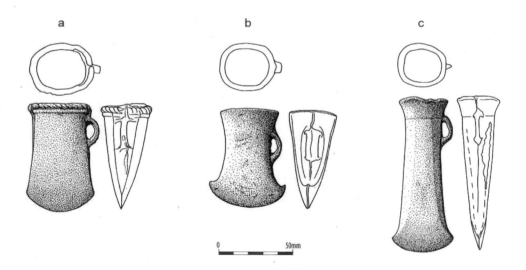

Land versus water in prehistory:
logboats on the ancient Tay

While the Tay Estuary would have been a major obstacle to land transport in prehistory and may well have marked a border, as today, it would have acted as a conduit for water transport from the coast inland along the rivers Tay and Earn. Coincidentally, the earliest preserved wheel from Scotland, made of ash and discovered in 1830 in the peat of Blair Drummond Moss, is broadly contemporary with the Carpow boat, having produced a date of 1255-815 BC. With no widespread network of roads and a largely wooded landscape, it is likely that wheeled vehicles, such as carts and wagons, were used over relatively short distances. Conversely, water offered a medium for extended transport and communication both around the estuary, and east to west from the sea deep inland along both Strathearn and up Strathtay. Indeed, the power of the tidal flow would have carried vessels well in land, as far as Almondbank in the Tay and west along the Earn well past Bridge of Earn. The 10m long Carpow logboat, around 0.8m wide would have weighed in the region of 1,500kg, and with an internal volume of around 3.5m^3, could have carried a crew of up to 14, sitting in single file and paddling on alternate sides of the boat. Alternatively, with a minimal crew of two, it could have carried around 10 passengers or around 900kg of cargo. While the records of at least eight logboats from the Tay estuary indicate the suitability of this type of craft to the shallow sheltered waters that exist there, logboats were not sea-going vessels. Their relative instability would have constrained their use largely to hugging the land with voyages over open water being dependant on ideal tidal and weather conditions.

Logboats can be powered by sail and more recently by outboard motor, but most commonly through paddling, rowing and punting. Paddling and rowing involve the use of paddles and oars, respectively, which contact only the water; while in punting the pole contacts with the river or estuary bed to propel the vessel forward. The difference between paddling and rowing is that rowing requires a mechanical connection between the oar and boat, while with paddling the paddles are hand-held. There are many ways in which the boat may have been used: as a working boat for fishing and wild-fowling, or as a barge or ferry for transporting cargo and people...

What was it used for?

A rich and varied array of natural resources would have been abundant throughout the Tay estuary in prehistoric times. Not all of the potential uses of the logboat relate to exploitation of these resources, however, as its capacity to transport cargo and people cannot be underestimated.

The Tay is renowned for its salmon; and fishing as a whole would have been a major resource exploited through line and net fishing, and probably the use of fish traps. There is understandably no archaeological evidence for lines and nets, and while stationary fish traps have not as yet been recognised on the Tay Estuary, they are widely recorded at similar estuaries throughout Britain and Ireland. These would have taken the form of baskets, perhaps fed with upright wattle walls to form a weir, strategically positioned in the inter-tidal to collect fish during ebb tides. The trapped fish would have been collected at low tide the use of small boats at slack water would offer an excellent method of transporting the catch, rather than walking often long distances across mudflats. Indeed, accessing the low inter-tidal zone would also reveal a variety of shellfish. The numerous round-woods and carpentry waste found inside the logboat would fit perfectly with both basketry and wattle making. In addition, the Tay Estuary has long been noted for its variety and frequency of wild-fowl and again exploiting this valuable resource would no doubt have been as popular in prehistory, if not more, than it still is today. While now less common, both grey and common seals visit the estuary today, and were widely hunted, although by 1850, the sale of five seals in Perth was being described as a 'curiosity'. In prehistory, the oil and skins of seals would have been a resource not easily obtained from surrounding environments. It is even possible that salt was being extracted from sea water on the Tay, as is first recognised in the Late Bronze Age along the Essex coast, where natural pools, in which the sun evaporated sea-water, were gradually modified with shallow artificial clay lined tanks. While there is currently no evidence for this industry on the Tay, it may well have occurred, as all of the conditions required were ideal. In all of the above cases, the logboat would have proved an invaluable way to move around the estuary and transport goods: the alternative being access across salt-marsh, reed-beds and muddy creeks which, even with the provision of timber walkways would have been onerous.

With a crew of two, the Carpow boat could have carried a maximum cargo of around one tonne significant distances around the estuary and up and down the rivers over short periods of time with minimal effort. Moving to and from the estuary inland along both the Tay and the Earn, products from one environment could be transported to another, including stone, timber, wheat grain, reeds, peat and carcasses, in addition to the estuarine products above. There is evidence for logboats carrying cargo, such as the Shardlow boat with its five large blocks of quarried stone found a few kilometres upstream from its source on the River Trent.

An artist's reconstruction of the logboat transporting goods along the River Earn.

Finally, the potential of Carpow for transporting people around key parts of the landscape is illustrated by ferry sites which operated until the 19th century AD. As the boat could have carried as many as 14 people safely, this simple function may have been the boats primary occupation. It is striking that the find-spot of the boat is in such close proximity to the Ferryfield of Carpow and what would have been one of the busiest crossing points in the medieval period.

An artist's reconstruction of the logboat transporting people across the River Tay .

A Bronze Age vessel brought to life

A link in the chain - one boat among many...

There would undoubtedly have been many smaller craft in use on both the estuary and the rivers, including smaller logboats and skin and possibly reed built vessels. It is also possible, however, that the Carpow boat operated alongside much larger, more capacious sewn-plank boats, evidenced in Britain at this time through 11 examples from the Humber region, the Severn Estuary and Dover. These were also made of oak, date from around 1900 BC to 400 BC, and offered increased volume and stability. While it is still debated as to whether they crossed the English Channel, they would certainly have been able to hug the coastline outside the estuary, outwith the reach of logboats such as Carpow. Broadly contemporary vessels such as the Dover (1550 BC) and Brigg (800 BC) boats were in the region of 15m in length, 2-3m in breadth and able to carry a cargos of around 5-6 tonnes.

To the Bronze Age people living near water, boats would have been an everyday experience, and it is likely smaller logboats and other craft were constructed by individuals from within one family and that the skills and techniques required were widely known. The manufacture of these larger sewn-plank boats is likely to have required specialist advisors and tradesmen, however, and probably the cooperation of several extended families, possibly reflecting a larger local political unit. The Carpow boat, requiring a team of five or six, and possibly as many as 10 to 12 at some stages, could have been undertaken by an extended family, possibly with additional support required at times.

In light of the likelihood of a network of watercraft of different sizes, the question of longer distance movement of materials should also be considered, as the Tay itself, as a key east coast inlet, was part of a much larger system of coastal and riverine routes including the Firth of Forth, the Humber and the Thames. South of this, contact was ultimately made with the near-Continent, but also importantly east-west along the south coast, to Cornwall, Wales and Ireland beyond. One ultimate material requiring transportation in the period is bronze. There was clearly significant movement of bronze itself, and the copper and tin required to make it, from the Middle Bronze Age onwards. Generally, the raw materials for bronze required importing from the far west of Britain, Ireland or the Continent, and it is possible to envisage larger plank-sewn vessels, travelling greater distances, hugging the coasts, and decanting materials to be transported further inland on rivers by logboats like Carpow.

A final thought

The Late Bronze Age metalwork from the Tay clearly indicates that the river was the focus of ritual activity associated with the deposition of swords and other metalwork between what is now Perth and Mugdrum Island. This should come as no surprise given the importance of this mighty river, and indeed this ritual dimension may well have its origins in the economic value and importance of the river in terms of communication and transport. The dramatic view of the river at Moncreiffe Island, set beneath the near vertical cliffs of Kinnoull Hill, was clearly a special place then, as now, and the recovery of the Carpow logboat from where this river ends, and meets it partner the Earn, to become the open estuary, is significant. Around the estuary, ritual monuments such as stone circles and standing stones were set on higher ground above the lower-lying wetlands surrounding the estuary. While no direct association can be made, a possible ritual aspect to Carpow should also be considered, as there are examples where logboats clearly have been ritually deposited. At Fiskerton, Lincolnshire, a votive deposition has been interpreted for one of two logboats recently excavated at an Iron Age timber causeway. The vessel was apparently deposited in pristine condition and set between two clusters of posts and pegged into position. A large assemblage of other artefacts interpreted as votive offerings were discovered, including a sword, an iron dagger, a spear, numerous pieces of bronze and a socketted axe, the latter being a copy of Late Bronze Age examples. With a ritual focus demonstrated for this section of the Tay it is possible, if not likely that logboats were involved, even if not as their primary function. Indeed, given the example of Fiskerton, then deliberate sinking of the vessel, at some point, cannot be ruled out.

The significance of the Carpow vessel is not only its early date and good state of preservation, but the fact that it is one of a very few Scottish logboats to be recorded, and recovered and conserved using modern techniques of archaeology and conservation. In addition to its contributions to logboat studies, this artefact has allowed a long overdue review of our understanding of the Late Bronze Age of the area, and in particular the relationship between the land and the waterways. Ultimately we can only ponder options for how the natural resources of the estuary were exploited and distributed, both at a subsistence level and as a generator of 'wealth'. While it may be possible that craft such as Carpow provided a floating platform from which votive offerings were cast into the river; we should not consider such ideas without closing our minds to more prosaic explanations.

Further Reading

Clark, P (ed) 2004 *The Dover Bronze Age Boat*, Swindon.

Clark, P 2009 *Bronze Age Connections: Cultural contact in Prehistoric Europe*, Oxford: Oxbow Books.

Coutts H 1971 *Tayside before History*. Dundee Museum and Art Gallery.

Fry, M F 2000 *Coití Logboats from Northern Ireland*. Northern Ireland Archaeological Monographs 4, Antrim.

McGrail, S 1987 *Ancient boats in NW Europe: the archaeology of water transport to AD 1500*. London.

Millett, M and McGrail, S 1987 The Archaeology of the Hasholme Logboat, *Archaeological Journal* 144, 69-155.

Mowat, R J C 1996 *The Logboats of Scotland, With Notes on Related Artefact Types*. Oxbow monograph 68, Oxford.

Strachan, D 2010 *Carpow in Context: A Late Bronze Age Logboat from the Tay*. Society of Antiquaries of Scotland.

About the Author

A graduate of Cardiff University, David has worked for over 20 years as an archaeologist for both local and national government in Wales, England and Scotland. He has specialised in the uses of air photography and in inter-tidal archaeology, and has worked with Perth and Kinross Heritage Trust, of which he is now Manager, since 2000.

Acknowledgements

This publication is a distilled version of a series of papers and studies first presented at a conference entitled *Tales of the Riverbank: the Carpow Bronze Age logboat in context*, held at Abernethy in September 2007. These, and other studies, were subsequently developed into the full publication of the Carpow project: the monograph, in preparation at the time of writing, published by the Society of Antiquaries of Scotland. The contributors are, in alphabetical order: Peter Clark, Gordon Cook, Trevor Cowie, Mike Cressey, Anne Crone, Sue Dawson, Damian Goodburn, Mark Hall, Seán McGrail, Paula Milburn, Robert Mowat, Rob Sands, Theo Skinner, Steven Timoney, Richard Tipping and Sarah Winlow. I am indebted to them all for their contributions and also to David Hogg and Leeanne Whitelaw for their excellent illustrations, used extensively within these pages.

The Carpow project was funded by Perth and Kinross Heritage Trust (PKHT) and Historic Scotland (HS) with in-kind contributions from the National Museums of Scotland (NMS) and Perth Museum and Art Gallery (PMAG). I am grateful to owners of Carpow bank, the Millar brothers of Jamesfield Farm, who gave us permission to excavate. The project itself was multi-disciplinary, and the expertise of the project's contracted partners, CFA Archaeology and Moorings & Marine Services was essential to the success of the venture, and particular thanks are due to Bruce Glendinning (CFA) and Jim Ferguson (MMS) who jointly, and ably, aided the author as project director. Thanks also to the (often very muddy) excavation and recovery team, again in alphabetical order: Ricky Blake, Jane Clark, Mike Cressey, Alasdair Curtis, Keith Emerson, Lindsay Farquharson, Mark Hall, Colleen Healey, Donny and Scott Macleod, Fiona MacKenzie, Scott McGuckin, Len McKinney, Chris O'Connell, Alison Sheridan, Jake Streatfeild-James, Steven Timoney and Sarah Winlow.

The Loch Tay project was funded by PKHT and was carried out in partnership with Scottish Crannog Centre who provided the site at Dalerb and the logs, which had been acquired through Big Tree Country connections: my thanks go to Barrie Andrian and Nick Dixon, and all other 'crannog staff', for their input throughout the project. The work was carried out under the instruction of ancient wood-working expert Damian Goodburn, who had previously made several logboats and was invaluable in unravelling the mysteries of how Carpow had been manufactured. His enthusiasm for passing on some of the fruits of his years of experience was much appreciated by both Trust staff and the volunteer team, made up of local residents, archaeology students and members of the 'bush-craft' fraternity. While some were present for only a couple of days and others camped on site for almost the full three weeks, their enthusiasm and energy was the key to success, whether while explaining their work to the public, mucking in with cooking, or in dealing with blisters and the memorable rain. They are: Clive Ashton Clements, Liam Clancy, Iain Connolly, Dominika Czop, Bruce Glendinning, Adam Harrison, Rachel Haworth, Atholl Houston, Scott Johnston, Michael Kelly, Amy Maitland-Gardner, John Minkin, John McCrone, Andy O'Neill, Callum Petrie, Tony Simpson, Tom Sneddon, Jake Streatfeild-James, Steve Timoney, Sarah Winlow and Vivienne Whyte.

Finally, I am as ever grateful to the Trustees of PKHT for their continual support throughout both projects and subsequent publications: a process which has evolved over a decade since I first stepped onto the mudflats at Carpow.